Securitized Real Estate and 1031 Exchanges

I0475863

This 32 page handbook addresses:

I.   What is Securitized Real Estate?

II.   What is a 1031 Exchange?

III.   What is a Delaware Statutory Trust (DST)?

IV.   Related Topics

What is Securitized Real Estate?

Securitized real estate is a real estate interest that is packaged and sold as a security. It is regulated by Federal and state securities law and requires more disclosure than most real estate offerings.

Real estate has the well-known advantage of depreciation and it also usually provides income as well as the potential for appreciation. When real estate is offered in the form of securities, investors must be given a professionally prepared private placement memorandum (PPM) as well as other offering documents. These offering documents must reflect due diligence appropriate to a securities offering. Typically, these are larger, institutional grade investments, managed by experienced sponsors.

What due diligence is performed?

Due diligence, or the analysis of the facts and circumstances associated with an investment, provides investors full disclosure of the facts and risks before they arrive at an investment decision. Initial due diligence will be performed by the sponsor, the lender, legal counsel, and then by a broker/dealer or other securities licensee.

Due diligence includes: 1) examination of the sponsor); 2) analysis of the properties; 3) analysis of the market; and 4) review of the structure of the project. If a 1031 transaction is contemplated, there will also be analysis of 1031 tax compliance

Reasons for rejection of a real estate offering by securities professionals vary; the property, the sponsor, the financing, or the market--each may be judged problematic.

Advantages of Securitized Real Estate

Access to institutional grade investment properties

Securitized real estate offers accredited investors the opportunity to join with other accredited investors to own investment-grade real estate. Normally, these properties are financially secure, with creditworthy tenants under long-term triple net (NNN) leases, and under professional management. Asset classes include multifamily housing, NNN retail properties, office buildings, industrial complexes and warehouses, and hotels

Management free

Real estate professionals structure the property acquisition, maintain and lease the property, collect rent, service the mortgage, and eventually sell the property.

Combined with the 1031 exchange process, such a portfolio can grow tax-deferred over a number of years.

Income and appreciation

Investment-grade properties typically offer stable cash flow from rental income, paid monthly or quarterly. As the debt is serviced, the investor's equity in the property increases even if the value of the property does not. Also there is the potential for appreciation.

Tax-Sheltered Cash Flow

Some of the cash flow from these investments can be tax-sheltered and/or tax deferred by depreciation pass-through and interest deductions.

If an investor has held a property where the depreciation deductions have run out, or will do so soon, a 1031 exchange gives the investor an opportunity to restore these deductions in a replacement property if the DST or TIC has more debt than the debt on the investor's property. The additional debt offers a new tax basis to the investor—resulting in greater depreciation expense to shelter rental income from Federal and state taxes.

Many DST/TIC properties are leveraged with up to 75% non-recourse debt financing.

Diversification

With minimum investment requirements as low as $100,000 for a 1031 exchange, investors hedge risk by diversifying their real estate portfolio to include multiple properties in different geographic locations, as well as in different asset classes such as residential apartment complexes, retail shopping centers, office buildings, and industrial parks.

What are the risks of securitized real estate?

All investment real estate can have substantial risks, such as no guaranteed income, lack of liquidity, possible conflicts of interest with managers and affiliated persons or entities, risks associated with leverage, declining markets, and challenging economic conditions. The ultimate risk of investing in real estate is the total loss of the investment.

What is a 1031 Exchange?

Under IRS section 1031, an investor can defer capital gains tax and depreciation recapture by reinvesting the proceeds from the sale of investment property into replacement property.

1031 exchange tax deferrals can be continued through as many exchanges as the investor wishes. Of course if at any time the investor sells the property without reinvesting in a new property, there is capital gains and depreciation recapture.

In addition to tax deferral, a 1031 exchange permits investors to purchase a leveraged replacement property and thus increase their basis in the amount of additional debt assumed. This allows for additional depreciation pass-through which can shelter as much as 50% to 60% of the rental income cash flow.

On an after tax basis, the rate of return (ROR) for a 1031 exchange into securitized real estate is comparable to RORs on investments with significantly more risk. With any additional return from appreciation of the property, the after-tax return on investment on an annualized basis can be even greater.

Some of the most important requirements for an IRS approved 1031 exchange:

- **The exchange process must be facilitated by a Qualified Intermediary:**

The Qualified Intermediary (QI) is the professional responsible for the mechanics and process of an exchange. It holds the proceeds from the relinquished property until reinvested in the exchange property.

An "exchange agreement" must exist in writing between the QI and the investor to prevent the investor from having "constructive receipt" of the funds during the exchange period. The use of a qualified intermediary as an independent party to facilitate a tax-deferred exchange is a safe harbor established by Treasury Regulations.

- **The properties must be "like-kind":**

Virtually all real estate properties, whether raw land or with substantial improvements, qualify as like-kind. REITs, real estate funds, or other securities do not qualify for 1031 exchanges. Types of like-kind properties include:

Raw Land

Multi-Family Rentals

Single-Family Rentals

Retail Shopping Centers

Office Buildings

Industrial Facilities

Storage facilities

Rules for a 1031 exchange must be followed:

- The investor must identify in writing the exchange properties *within 45 days* of closing on the relinquished property in accordance under one of the following:
    - Three-Property Rule: Identification of up to three properties regardless of the value of property identified
    - 200% Rule: Identification of any number of properties wherein the combined FMV (fair market value) does not exceed 200% of the relinquished properties' FMV
    - 95% Rule: Identification of any number of properties regardless of the aggregate FMV, as long as at least 95% of the property is ultimately acquired.
- The investor must close on the replacement property or properties *within 180 days* of the closure of the relinquished property.

The properties must be held in a business or for the purpose of investment. The replacement property must be of equal or greater value than the relinquished property. The equity of the replacement property must be of equal or greater value than the equity of the relinquished property. The debt held by the replacement property must be of equal or greater value than the debt held by the relinquished property.

All net profit from the relinquished property must be used in the purchase of the replacement property.

Ownership Structures Used for 1031 Exchanges

The two most common ownership structures for 1031 exchanges are a Delaware Statutory Trust (DST) and a Tenancy in Common (TIC). Both of these structures can be used to hold like-kind interests in real estate for the purpose of a 1031 exchange.

The tenancy-in-common structure dates from earliest common law and was the traditional vehicle for multiple-owner 1031 exchanges in the US. In the last 10 years, however, most exchangers have begun to use the DST structure because it is simpler and more flexible.

Both DSTs and TICs are available as turnkey, pre-packaged investments, with management and non-recourse financing in place. They both offer superior efficiencies in the identification, acquisition, financing, and operating stages of real estate ownership. These efficiencies are especially helpful given the strict time restrictions when using a 1031 tax-deferred exchange.

In addition to DSTs and TICs, investors seeking real estate for the purpose of a 1031 exchange can consider oil and gas offerings or direct ownership of NNN leased properties. While most oil and gas programs are not viable for a 1031 exchange, some are designed specifically for this purpose.

An investor may find direct ownership of a NNN leased property more suitable. While not securitized offerings, NNN leased properties are often attractive to investors seeking to own a piece of high quality retail real estate with just a few other owners.

1031 Exchange Guidelines

Advanced planning is necessary and particular attention must be given to the timing of the sale of the relinquished property. The property owner must satisfy equity and debt replacement objectives to avoid boot. The IRS will not honor the exchange if either the 45-day identification period is missed or if replacement property is not acquired within the 180 day exchange period.

If a property owner finds an ideal replacement property before the relinquished property is sold, he may have to negotiate a reverse exchange; i.e., buy before selling. The IRS provides guidance on this type of reverse exchange in Revenue Procedure 2000-37. A reverse exchange requires the replacement property or the relinquished property to be parked with an "exchange accommodator titleholder" for 180 days pending the successful completion of the exchange.

Caveats:

- Trading down in total value? You are potentially taxable to the extent of the trade-down.
- Trading down in equity? You are potentially taxable to the extent of the trade-down.
- Depreciation Recapture

Capital gain tax rates are currently low, but tax rules require investors to recapture at a high tax rate, typically 25%, on the portion of the gain that relates to allowable depreciation over the period the asset was held. Depreciation recapture is a significant factor in motivating an investor to participate in a like-kind exchange.

If an investor's marginal income tax bracket is greater than 15%, and the real estate sold is the only business asset sold in the tax year of the sale, the tax should not be higher than 15%.

The gain from the sale by a non-corporate taxpayer of real estate that is a capital asset, or is used in a business, and is held more than 12 months, is not normally taxed at a rate higher than 15%.

When the asset sold is depreciable real estate, a maximum rate of 25% applies to "non-recaptured Section 1250 gain" and a maximum rate of 15% applies to the balance of the gain. Non-recaptured Section 1250 gain refers to the portion of gain that is eligible for capital gains treatment even though it is attributable to previously allowable depreciation.

Property placed in service after 1986

For real estate placed in service after 1986, all depreciation deductions allowable before the sale of the real estate give rise to non-recaptured section 1250 gain.

Property placed in service between 1981 and 1986

For real estate placed in service after 1980 but before 1987, the treatment of gain on sale depends on whether the real estate is residential or non-residential.

Page9

Residential

Depreciated residential pre-1987 real estate, using straight-line depreciation, results in the same tax consequence as for a sale of post-1987 property, as described above. If you used a declining balance method to depreciate the real estate, the gain on the sale would be taxed as follows:

- Gain, to the extent of the depreciation claimed that exceeds what would have been allowable under straight-line depreciation, will be recaptured as ordinary income, and taxed at rates as high as 35% (ordinary income rates), but the amount of excess depreciation subject to recapture may be less for certain low-income housing.
- Gain, to the extent of the depreciation that is not recaptured as ordinary income, will be taxed at a rate of 25%.
- The balance of the gain will be taxed at a rate of 15%.

Non-residential

As is the case for residential pre-1987 real estate, if you depreciated non-residential pre-1987 real estate using just straight-line depreciation, the tax results when you sell it will be the same as for a sale of post-1986 property, as described above. But if you used a declining-balance method to depreciate, the gain on sale would be taxed as follows:

- Gain, to the extent of the full amount of depreciation allowable to the time of sale, is recaptured as ordinary income, and taxed at ordinary income rates;
- The balance of the gain is taxed at 15%.

Pre-1981 Property

The following rules apply if you sell real estate placed in service before 1981:

- The excess of depreciation claimed over straight-line depreciation is recaptured as ordinary income, and thus taxed at ordinary income rates (but the amount of excess depreciation subject to recapture may be less for certain residential real estate or for real estate acquired before 1970).
- Gain, to the extent of the balance of depreciation allowable, is non-recaptured Section 1250 gain, taxed at a rate of 25%.
- The balance of the gain, if any, would be taxed at a rate of 15%.

Ownership Structures Used for 1031 Exchanges

The two most common ownership structures are a Delaware Statutory Trust (DST) and a Tenancy in Common (TIC). Both of these structures can qualify as a like-kind interest in real estate for the purposes of a 1031 exchange.

The tenancy-in-common structure dates from earliest common law and was the traditional vehicle for multiple-owner 1031 exchanges in the US. In the last 10 years, however, most people have been using the DST structure, which is both simpler and more flexible.

Both DSTs and TICs are available as turnkey, pre-packaged investments, with management and non-recourse financing in place. They both offer superior efficiencies in the identification, acquisition, financing, and operating stages of real estate ownership. These efficiencies are especially helpful given the strict time restrictions when using a 1031 tax-deferred exchange.

In addition to DSTs and TICs, investors seeking to purchase real estate for the purpose of a 1031 exchange can consider the options of oil and gas offerings or direct ownership of NNN leased properties. While most oil and gas programs are not viable for 1031 exchange, some are designed for this purpose. Lastly, an investor may find direct ownership of a NNN leased property most suitable. While not securitized offerings, NNN leased properties are often attractive to investors seeking to own a piece of high quality retail real estate themselves, or together with one or two other owners.

Changing how title to your property is being held or dissolving partnerships during the exchange may cause the exchange to be dishonored due to holding-period issues.

Two cautions

- If you are trading down in total value, you are potentially taxable to the extent of the trade-down;
- If you are trading down in equity, you are potentially taxable to the extent of the trade-down.

Depreciation Recapture

Capital gain tax rates are currently low, but tax rules require investors to recapture at a higher tax rate (typically 25%) the portion of the gain on the sale that relates to allowable depreciation over the period the asset was held. Depreciation recapture is a significant factor in motivating an investor to participate in a like-kind exchange.

If an investor's marginal income tax bracket is greater than 15%, and the real estate sold is the only business asset sold in the tax year of the sale, the tax should not be higher than 15%.

Generally, the gain from the sale by a non-corporate taxpayer of real estate that is a capital asset, or is used in a business, and is held more than 12 months, is not taxed at a rate higher than 15%.

However, when the asset sold is depreciable real estate, a maximum rate of 25% will apply to "non-recaptured Section 1250 gain" and a maximum rate of 15% will apply to the balance of the gain .Non-recaptured Section 1250 gain refers to the portion of gain that is eligible for capital gains treatment even though it is attributable to previously allowable depreciation. A further complication is that the portion of the gain that is non-recaptured Section 1250 gain depends, as discussed below, on when the property was placed in service.

Property placed in service after 1986

For real estate placed in service after 1986, all depreciation deductions give rise to non-recaptured section 1250 gain.

Property placed in service between 1981 and 1986

For real estate placed in service after 1980 but before 1987, the treatment of gain on sale depends on whether the real estate is residential or non-residential.

Residential Real Estate

Depreciated residential pre-1987 real estate, using straight-line depreciation, results in the same tax consequence as with a sale of post-1987 property, as described above. If a declining balance method is used to depreciate the real estate, the gain on sale would be taxed as follows:

- Gain, to the extent of the depreciation claimed that exceeds what would have been allowable under straight-line depreciation, will be recaptured as ordinary income, and taxed at rates as high as 35% in 2003 and later years (ordinary income rates), but the amount of excess depreciation subject to recapture may be less for certain low-income housing.
- Gain, to the extent of the depreciation that is not recaptured as ordinary income, will be taxed at a rate of 25%.
- The balance of the gain will be taxed at a rate of 15%.

Non-residential Real Estate

As is the case for residential pre-1987 real estate, if you depreciated non-residential pre-1987 property using straight-line depreciation, the tax results if you sell it will be the same as for a sale of post-1986 property. But if you used a declining-balance method to depreciate, the gain on sale would be taxed as follows:

- Gain, to the extent of the full amount of depreciation allowable to the time of sale, would be recaptured as ordinary income, and, thus, taxed at ordinary income rates;
- The balance of the gain would be taxed at a rate of 15%.

Pre-1981 Property

The following rules apply if you sell real estate placed in service before 1981:

- The excess of depreciation claimed over straight-line depreciation is recaptured as ordinary income, and thus taxed at ordinary income rates (but the amount of excess depreciation subject to recapture may be less for certain residential real estate or for real estate acquired before 1970).
- Gain, to the extent of the balance of depreciation allowable, is unrecaptured Section 1250 gain, taxed at a rate of 25%.
- The balance of the gain, if any, would be taxed at a rate of 15%.

If you have further questions about the above rules, or would like to compute the potential tax that you face, please contact your tax advisor.

What is a Delaware Statutory Trust?

A Delaware Statutory Trust (DST) is a separate legal entity created as a trust under Delaware statutory law. Investors in a DST own a pro rata interest in the trust and have the right to receive distributions from the operation of the trust, from rental income and from the eventual sale of the property. Investors do not have deeded title to the property; the trust has deed to the property and, through the signatory trustee, makes the decisions regarding the property. The beneficiaries of the trust have no authority over the day to day handling of the property or the timing and details of its eventual sale. While initially this may seem to be disadvantageous to the investor, this structure actually opens up the possibility for significant advantages

For the purposes of a 1031 tax-deferred exchange, the purchase of a beneficial interest in a DST is treated as a direct interest in real estate, satisfying that requirement of IRS Revenue Ruling 2004-86.

An IRS Revenue Ruling, dissimilar to an IRS Revenue Procedure, may be relied upon by other taxpayers in defense of a 1031 exchange position.

A DST can also be an attractive investment vehicle for investors even without the 1031 exchange. Because it is a direct interest in real estate the investor can conduct a 1031 tax deferred exchange if and when the property is sold, thus beginning the cycle of tax deferred real estate ownership at that time.

Due to legal limitations and the nature of DST financing, the use of a DST is generally limited to: a) long-term "A" credit, triple-net leased properties, and b) properties leased to an affiliate of the sponsor (master tenant) who operates the property on a triple-net basis (master lease).

A Delaware Statutory Trust is similar to a unit investment trust. Securities or real estate are purchased for the trust and held until such a time as the proceeds are distributed to the investors. The trust is not considered a taxable entity so all profits and losses are passed through.

The concept for business trusts, especially those that involve the holding of property, dates back to early English common law. With the passage of the Delaware Statutory Trust Act in 1988, statutory trusts can be legal entities separate from their trustees. The act allows the trustees to structure the entity in a way that is most beneficial to the relationship of all parties while offering liability protection similar to that of a limited liability company or partnership.

Delaware statutory trusts are being used as a form of tax deferral, asset protection, and balance sheet advantages in real estate securitization. For the purposes of owning a "direct interest in real estate," which is critical to qualify for a 1031 exchange, IRS Revenue Ruling 2004-86 opened the way for DSTs to become a common ownership structure. A beneficial interest in a DST which owns real estate is now considered a "direct interest in real estate" and thus qualifies for a 1031 exchange.

Risks of Delaware Statutory Trusts

The risks of investing in a DST include the risk of relying on the program sponsor; the risk of sponsor insolvency; and the risks associated with giving decision-making to any third party. If the property held by the DST is leveraged, there is the also the risk of being unable to re-finance the project at the end of the term of the loan. There is also the risk of conflicts of interest with program sponsors, trustees, property managers, or other affiliates.

In addition, there are tax-related risks when using a DST ownership structure for the purpose of a 1031 exchange. While the DST offerings are generally accompanied by a legal opinion that they are suitable for a 1031 exchange, there is no guarantee that the IRS will approve any given offering.

Benefits of a Delaware Statutory Trusts

In addition to other benefits of securitized real estate, DST investors enjoy the following:

No need for unanimous owner approval

Unanimous approval of the individual investors is not required to deal with unexpected, adverse developments. The signatory trustee is empowered to take necessary action, such as restructure financing or renegotiate leases.

Less expensive; easier financing

One advantage of the DST structure is that the lender deals with the trust as the only borrower, making it easier and less expensive to obtain financing. This is in contrast to a TIC arrangement where the lender needs to approve up to 35 different borrowers. Because the loan is obtained by the trust, there is no need for the individual investors to be qualified. Also, their participation in the trust does not affect their credit rating.

No fraud carve-outs

Since the investors' only right with respect to the DST is to receive distributions (they have no voting rights), investor fraud carve-outs are eliminated. The lender looks only to the sponsor with regard to carve-outs from the non-recourse provisions of the loan.

Lower minimum investment

Private placement DST offerings may have up to 499 investors so the minimum investment amounts are lower. Most DST sponsors will set arbitrary minimum investment levels to limit the number of investors to a manageable number, but investments can be as low as $25,000, although 1031 exchange minimums are often $100,000.

No Need for an LLC

DST investors do not have to pay annual state filing fees.

No trustee term time limit

The signatory trustee of the DST or one of the sponsor's affiliates will be the sponsor of the private placement offering. Unlike a TIC, there is no one-year time limit on the trusteeship or the term of the property manager. This gives the lender comfort that the sponsor will maintain involvement with the property.

No inadvertent termination

A DST has a Delaware trustee as required by statute so the trust cannot inadvertently terminate.

What is a tenancy in common?

Tenancy in common is a co-ownership structure under which multiple investors pool their funds to own one property. Each investor owns an undivided fractional interest and participates in a proportionate share of net income, tax shelters, and appreciation. Each owner receives a separate property deed and title insurance for their percentage interest in the property, and has all the same rights and privileges as a single, fee simple owner. Like a DST, the purchase of a TIC interest is treated as a direct interest in real estate, qualifying as "like kind" real estate for 1031 exchange purposes. However, because each TIC investor holds title, there may be the need to sign multiple "carve-outs" related to investor fraud and environmental issues.

Due to stricter underwriting standards, the recent trend has been to limit TIC offerings to all cash.

TIC investors typically set up limited liability corporations (LLCs) for the purpose of TIC ownership, providing another level of protection.

Financing issues

The DST structure has simplified the financing process for securitized real estate. It also offers the investor access to very competitive interest rates usually only available to institutions. The trust will own 100% fee interest in the real estate and is the sole borrower. Unlike a tenancy-in-common where there can be up to 35 individual borrowers, each of whom needs to be approved by the lender, with a DST the lender only makes one loan to one borrower.

A well-structured DST which owns investment-grade real estate can be attractive to institutional lenders due to a track record of the sponsor in property management, and because DSTs are bankruptcy remote. DST agreements contain special purpose entity provisions which prevent the bankruptcy creditors of the beneficiaries from reaching the DST's property. This assures the lender that it can foreclose on its first mortgage of the real estate should the need arise.

The lender does not need to underwrite or qualify any investors. Other than Patriot Act considerations, due diligence investigations of investors is normally not necessary. And if the sponsor only sells to accredited investors, the lender does not need to monitor transfers of beneficial interests.

The DST Master Lease

Tax law requires that the DST trustee is prohibited from taking certain actions with respect to leasing, financing and capital-raising. Since the beneficiaries have no control over the operations of the mortgaged property, either a master lease or a long-term triple-net lease to a credit tenant is required.

In the case of a master lease, the master tenant, who is generally an affiliate of the sponsor, will sublet the property to residential or commercial tenants. The master tenant also handles maintenance and repairs, or contracts with a management agent, often an affiliate of the sponsor.

The master tenant is empowered to do everything that an owner of the property would be empowered to do. Such master lease arrangements satisfy requirements of the law and are very attractive to institutional lenders because they eliminate the concern with how to ensure the unanimous consent of the tenants-in-common to management actions.

Special purpose entity structure

The master tenant is structured as a special purpose entity. This gives the lender more bankruptcy protection. Most master tenants are only minimally capitalized and the sponsors must have the requisite net worth and liquidity to satisfy lender requirements.

The master lease will generally provide for rent to be paid by the master tenant to the DST in a set amount equal to debt service plus a market rate of return. The master lease incentivizes the master tenant to maximize the mortgaged property's net operating income. The master tenant retains all net operating income over and above debt service and rent payments under the master lease. What is a 1031 Exchange?

Under IRS section 1031, an investor can defer capital gains tax and depreciation recapture by reinvesting the proceeds from the sale of investment property into replacement property.

1031 exchange deferrals can be continued through as many exchanges as the investor wishes. Of course, if at any time the investor sells the property without reinvesting in a new property, there will be capital gains and depreciation recapture and consequent tax liability.

Page 18

In addition to tax deferral, a 1031 exchange permits investors to purchase a leveraged replacement property and thus increase their basis. This allows for additional depreciation pass-through which can shelter as much as 50% to 60% of the rental income cash flow from income taxation.

On an after tax basis, the rate of return (ROR) for a 1031 exchange into securitized real estate is comparable to RORs on investments with significantly more risk. With additional return from appreciation of the property, the after-tax return on investment on an annualized basis is even greater.

Some of the most important requirements for an IRS approved 1031 exchange:

The exchange process must be facilitated by a qualified intermediary:

The qualified intermediary (QI) is the professional responsible for the mechanics and process of an exchange. It holds the proceeds from the relinquished property until reinvested in the exchange property.

An "exchange agreement" must exist in writing between the QI and the investor to prevent the investor from having "constructive receipt" of the funds during the exchange period. The use of a qualified intermediary as an independent party to facilitate a tax-deferred exchange is a safe harbor established by Treasury Regulations.

The properties must be "like-kind." Virtually all real estate properties, whether raw land or with substantial improvements, will qualify as like-kind. Securities offered by REITs, real estate funds, or other securities, do not qualify for 1031 exchanges. Types of like-kind properties include:

- Raw Land

- Multi-Family Rentals

- Single-Family Rentals

- Retail Shopping Centers

- Office Buildings

- Industrial Facilities

- Storage facilities

Rules

The investor must identify in writing exchange properties within 45 days of the closure of the relinquished property, as follows:

Three-Property Rule: Identification of up to three properties regardless of the total value of property identified

200% Rule: Identification of any number of properties wherein the combined FMV (fair market value) does not exceed 200% of the relinquished properties' FMV

95% Rule: Identification of any number of properties regardless of the aggregate FMV, as long as at least 95% of the property is ultimately acquired

The investor must close on the replacement property or properties within 180 days of the closure of the relinquished property.

The properties must be held either for productive use in a business or for the purpose of investment.

The replacement property must be of equal or greater value than the relinquished property.

The equity of the replacement property must be of equal or greater value than the equity of the relinquished property.

The debt held by the replacement property must be of equal or greater than the debt held by the relinquished property.

All net profit from the relinquished property must be used in the purchase of the replacement property. This incentivizes the master tenant to cover short-term operating deficits, if necessary.

Self-reserve

Sponsors self-reserve from net operating income, over and above typical lender replacement reserves, for unanticipated repairs and uninsured losses.

The investors have no vote in the operations of the property and there is usually no need for them to sign any non-recourse loan carve-outs. As with the primary loan, the lender deals directly with the trust on the matter of carve-outs. Standard carve-outs for environmental damages and investor fraud are executed by the DST trustee, according the DST investor an absolute non-recourse loan. The DST investor is not personally liable for the repayment (non-recourse) of the loan, and the loan does not affect the investor's personal credit report.

DST trust agreement restrictions

IRS Revenue Ruling 2004-86, which forms the basis for a DST transaction in a Section 1031 exchange program, has prohibitions on the powers of the trustee. These restrictions must be incorporated into the trust agreement.

Prohibited Activities

- There can be no future contributions to the DST by either current or new beneficiaries.
- The trustee cannot renegotiate the terms of the existing loans and cannot borrow any new funds from any party unless a loan default exists following a tenant bankruptcy or insolvency.
- The trustee cannot reinvest the proceeds from the sale of the real estate.
- The trustee is limited to making capital expenditures with respect to the property for normal repair and maintenance, minor non-structural capital improvements, and those required by law.
- Any reserves or cash held between distribution dates can only be invested in short-term debt obligations.
- All cash other than necessary reserves must be distributed on a current basis.
- The trustee cannot enter into new leases or renegotiate the current leases, unless there is a tenant bankruptcy or insolvency.

Because of these IRS restrictions, the only forms of a real estate transaction that make sense in a DST are a master lease transaction, whereby the master tenant takes on all of the operating responsibilities, or a triple net long-term lease to an "A" credit tenant. The sponsor should also attempt to mitigate against the effect of these seven prohibitions by:

- Acquiring only new or recently rehabilitated Class A properties

- Raising substantial funds for capital reserves in the offering
- Having financing terms which go out 7 to 10 years, but are shorter than the terms of the master lease
- Planning for the sale of the property prior to the maturity date of the loan.

The Springing LLC

If the loan is endangered a provision in the trust agreement should provide that if the trustee determines that the DST is in danger of losing the mortgaged property due to default on the loan, and tax-related restrictions limit the trustee's ability to act, Delaware law permits conversion to a LLC by a simple election which does not constitute a transfer under Delaware law.

This "springing LLC" will permit the raising of additional funds, the raising of new financing or renegotiation of the terms of the existing financing, and the renegotiation of leases. In addition, it will provide that the trustee (or sponsor) will become the manager of the LLC with full operating control.

Summary

Various financing sources have embraced the DST structure. A steady market has been developing for DSTs. They are much less complex than the structure of TIC transactions, they shield investors from liabilities with respect to the mortgaged property, and they remove the investors from involvement in operation of the property.

Related Topics

Private Placement Memorandum

Securitized real estate offerings are SEC Rule 506 exempt offerings regulated under the 1933 Securities Act. They require the sponsor to provide a private placement memorandum (PPM) to investors. The PPM is a detailed description of the property, the sponsor, and financial details (including projected return on the investment). The PPM will include due diligence reports, leases, and contracts, as well as a discussion of the risks.

A qualified expert must opine on whether the offering, as structured, meets the provisions for IRS Revenue Ruling 2004-86 or Revenue Procedure 2002-22 and qualifies for 1031 exchange treatment.

Each accredited investor must be given a copy of the PPM and other offering documents before making a decision to invest.

Direct Investments

Direct investments in real estate include real estate investment trusts (REITs), real estate private funds, and oil & gas royalty programs. None of these are eligible for 1031 exchanges. Direct ownership of a triple net leased property as well as some oil and gas royalty programs **are** eligible for a 1031 exchange.

These private placements are available only to accredited investors under SEC Rule 506. They are not publicly traded and should be considered illiquid. They require a private placement memorandum and other offering documents.

Real Estate Investment Trust (REIT)

A REIT is a corporation which invests in real estate, either properties or mortgages. An interest in a REIT is a security. REITs typically raise up to 1 billion dollars in capital and purchase a portfolio of properties over a period of several years. These properties produce rental income. A REIT must abide by specific rules. It is not required to pay corporate income taxes as long as it distributes at least 90 percent of its taxable income to shareholders annually. All dividend distributions made to investors are taxed only at the investor level, avoiding double taxation.

REITs can either be offered as private placement investments to accredited investors under the exemptions offered by Rule 506, or they can be publicly traded. The private offerings should be considered illiquid investments. One goal of many REITs is to be acquired by a larger REIT.

Types of REITs

Equity REITs buy and own properties and are measured by the equity or value of their real estate assets. Their revenue is in the form of rent.

Mortgage REITs buy and own property mortgages. These REITs lend money for mortgages to owners of real estate, or purchase existing mortgages or mortgage-backed securities. Their revenues are generated by the interest that they earn on the mortgage loans.

Hybrid REITs combine the strategies of equity REITs and mortgage REITs by investing in both properties and mortgages.

Real Estate Funds

Real estate funds are usually larger than DSTs or TICs but smaller than REITs. They often seek to raise up to $100 million to purchase income-producing real estate. Many funds use leverage to increase their purchasing ability and projected returns (and risk).

With a more manageable size (compared to REITs), real estate funds are able to focus on particular asset classes or regions of the country. Some funds will also focus on purchasing real estate from certain institutional sellers, allowing them access to discounts or benefits not normally available to the smaller investor.

Just as with DST or TIC offerings, real estate private funds typically have a projected period for holding the property, usually 5 to 7 years. The actual date of sale will depend upon a number of factors related to the specific property and to the overall market.

Investments in real estate funds are not considered an interest in real estate and are not eligible for 1031 exchange purposes.

As there is no established secondary market for these interests, they should be considered illiquid.

Oil & Gas Offerings

These interests lie underground and are commonly referred to as "subsurface interests." Subsurface interests are mineral rights.

There are two types of mineral rights.

One is a royalty interest, where landowners are entitled to a percentage of any extracted minerals from the efforts of others, contracted to enter the land for exploration and drilling.

The other kind of interest in mineral rights is called a working interest, giving exclusive authorization to enter the land to extract oil and gas--but with the land owners sharing in development and operating expenses as well as revenues.

Both working and royalty interest investment programs feature advantages similar to many DST and TIC investments, such as monthly cash flow, tax deferral, and a depreciation or depletion allowance.

In many oil and gas programs, there are no closing costs. These investments are not dependent on real estate values or rent collections. The opportunity to diversify out of real estate makes these programs appealing to some high net worth individuals interested in alternative class investments.

Some oil and gas programs are designed to meet the qualifications of "like-kind" replacement property, and are thus eligible for 1031 exchange purposes.

NNN Leased Properties

In addition to securitized real estate offerings, some investors purchase NNN leased investment-grade real estate directly. These properties produce both monthly income and have the potential for appreciation. They enjoy the tax benefits of real estate and they are eligible for 1031 exchanges.

An investment in a NNN leased property can be attractive for a larger investor who desires to have more direct input in the oversight of the property or who desires to own a property with just a few other investors.

Glossary for Securitized Real Estate and 1031 Exchanges

Accredited Investor

The SEC defines an accredited investor as an individual with either $1 million in net worth (all assets, excluding primary residence, less all liabilities) or net income for the last two years of $200,000 or greater ($300,000 if spouse has income) with a reasonable expectation of such earnings in the current year.

Basis (Cost Basis)

Basis is the original cost of property plus the cost of improvements, adjusted for depreciation. When property is sold, the taxpayer pays/saves taxes on a capital gain/loss that equals the amount realized on the sale minus the property's basis. Cost basis is needed because tax is due based on the gain in value of an asset. IRS Publication 551 reads: "Basis is the amount of your investment in property for tax purposes. Use the basis of property to figure depreciation, amortization, depletion, and casualty losses. Also use it to figure gain or loss on the sale or other disposition of property."

Boot

Boot is the face amount of money or debt and the fair market value of non-like-kind property received in an exchange. The fact that boot is received does not disqualify an exchange; the boot is, however, subject to capital gains tax to the extent of recognized gain on the sale of relinquished property.

Constructive Receipt

Income not actually received or possessed is "constructively received" and reportable if it is within the Exchanger's control.

Delaware Statutory Trust (DST)

A separate legal entity created as a trust under Delaware statutory law that permits a flexible approach to the design and operation of the entity to be used in in a Section 1031 exchange.

Depreciation Recapture

Depreciation recapture refers to the portion from the sale of a property which has been previously deducted as depreciation. If a property purchased for $100,000 is sold for $125,000 and during the time of ownership $50,000 was claimed as depreciation deductions, this $50,000 is depreciation recapture and taxed as such while the additional $25,000 would be considered capital gain and taxed at a different rate.

Direct Participation Program (DPP)

A business venture designed to let investors participate directly in the cash flow and tax benefits of the underlying investment. The DPP is generally a passive investment in a real estate or energy-related project. Also known as a "direct participation plan," DPPs are organized as limited partnerships, subchapter S corporations, or general partnership, and do not qualify for a 1031 exchange. While DST and TIC offerings are technically DPPs, they still qualify for a 1031 exchange.

Exchanger

This is a taxpayer seeking to defer capital gains tax under the provisions of IRC Section 1031 by means of a real estate exchange.

Exchange Period

The period of time in which the Exchanger must acquire title to replacement property to qualify under the safe harbor for the exchange. The period ends 180 days after the relinquished property is transferred or the due date (including extensions) of the Exchanger's federal income tax return for the year in which the Exchanger relinquished the property in the exchange, whichever is earlier.

Like-Kind Property

This refers to the nature and character of the property, not to its grade or quality. One class of property may not be exchanged, under Section 1031, for property of a different class or kind. As a general rule, as long as the purpose of the taxpayer is to hold the property as an investment, real property will be deemed like-kind with other real property. Real property cannot be exchanged for personal property.

Master Tenant

In a DST, the trust will often lease the entire property to a Master Tenant, who then subleases the property to the actual tenants. This allows the investors in a DST to have a direct interest in real estate; and it removes both the trust and the investors from the direct day-to-day management of the property and the subleases, which are the responsibility of the Master Tenant. The same results occur when the entire property of a DST is leased to one tenant on a NNN basis.

Mortgage Boot

This represents the liabilities assumed or taken subject to an exchange. It is not as recognizable as cash or other non-like-kind property. The taxpayer is considered to have received mortgage boot even if the buyer refinances the property as part of the exchange and used the proceeds to pay off the taxpayer's mortgage.

NNN Lease

A NNN Lease is a net lease, structured as a turnkey investment property. The tenant is responsible for paying the property tax, insurance, and maintenance. "NNN" stands for "Net-Net-Net" and is called "Triple Net."

The rent collected under a net lease is net of expenses. It therefore lower than rent charged under a gross lease. Net lease types include single net, double net, triple net and even bondable triple net leases. The term "net lease" is often used as a shorthand expression when referring to NNN leases.

Private Placement or Exempt Offering

Private placements are a way of raising money outside of public markets. The placement does not have to be registered with the SEC but it must qualify as an exempt offering under SEC Rule 506. Private placement offerings can be made to institutional investors or to accredited investors.

Property Boot

A taxpayer who receives money or non-qualifying property is considered to have received property boot.

Qualified Intermediary (QI)

A qualified intermediary is a third-party that facilitates a section 1031 exchange on behalf of the exchanger. The qualified intermediary will work under an agreement with the exchanger to take possession of proceeds from the escrow of the relinquished property and use those proceeds to fund the escrow of the replacement property. This is a tax safe harbor that avoids the exchanger from having constructive receipt of the funds.

Real Estate Fund (Private Equity Real Estate Fund)

A mutual fund which pools capital from investors and invests primarily in equity or debt of real estate in order to produce income and capital gains for its unit holders. These investments involve an active management strategy, releasing properties for development or extensive redevelopment. These funds typically have a limited life span, consisting of an investment period during which properties are acquired, and a holding period during which active asset management is carried out and the properties sold.

Real Estate Investment Trust (REIT)

A REIT is a corporation which invests in real estate either through properties or mortgages, sold as a security. REITs can raise unlimited amounts of capital and purchase a portfolio of properties over a period of years. A REIT must abide by specific rules and restrictions so that it is not required to pay corporate income taxes. All dividend distributions made by a REIT to its investors are taxed only at the investor level, thereby avoiding double taxation. REITs can either be offered as private placement investments to accredited investors or they can be registered with the SEC and offered publically.

Relinquished Property

The relinquished property, also known as the exchange property, is the property originally owned by the exchanger and sold by the exchanger in a like-kind exchange.

Replacement Property

This is the acquisition property or the property acquired by the exchanger in a like-kind exchange process.

Royalty

Royalties are payments for the use of an asset. Oil and gas royalties are paid based upon the amount of oil and gas produced from a lease. Oil and gas royalty interests are classified as real property and they may be bought and sold privately or through public forums, like other real estate.

Sponsor

The sponsor acquires the assets and offers a securitized real estate offering such as a DST, a TIC, a REIT, or a real estate fund. With DSTs, the sponsor will acquire the real estate, structure the trust, and make the private placement offering to accredited investors through one or more brokers. The sponsor will contract with the master tenant and professional management company, both of which are often affiliates of the sponsor.

Tenancy-in-Common (TIC)

A co-ownership structure under which an investor may own an undivided fractional interest in an entire property and participate in a proportionate share of the net income, tax shelters, and growth.

Undivided Fractional Interest

With the tenancy-in-common ownership structure, each tenant owns an undivided fractional interest. Each tenant owns a fraction of the property, but they do not own a particular part of the property, meaning a specific area or section. Instead, they have fractional ownership of the entire undivided property.

The author, Douglas Slain, is the managing partner of Private Placement Advisors LLC. He teaches online courses on equity and debt crowdfunding and private placements, and he has been involved with real estate securities for 40 years. Slain received his J.D. from Stanford Law School and taught there as a clinical adjunct law professor for one term.

LinkedIn: http://www.linkedin.com/privateplacementadvisors/

www.ingramcontent.com/pod-product-compliance
Lightning Source LLC
Chambersburg PA
CBHW070732180526
45167CB00004B/1724

9 781542 752244